SOME VOICES

BY JOE PENHALL

D1260843

★

★

DRAMATISTS
PLAY SERVICE
INC.

for Piet Penhall

SOME VOICES was first performed at the Royal Court Theatre Upstairs in association with the Royal National Theatre Studio in London, England, on September 15, 1994. It was directed by Ian Rickson; the set design was by Rae Smith; the lighting design was by Jim Simmons; the sound design was by Paul Arditti; and the original music was by Stephen Warbeck. The cast was as follows:

DAVE .... Lloyd Hutchinson
LAURA .... Anna Livia Ryan
RAY .... Lee Ross
IVES .... Tom Watson
PETE .... Ray Winstone

CHARACTERS

RAY, in his early twenties
LAURA, Irish, the same age
PETE, Ray's brother, in his early thirties
DAVE, Irish, the same age
IVES, around fifty

SETTING

The action takes place over a period of about
six weeks in west London.

NOTE

A forward slash (/) within a speech serves
as the cue for the next speaker to overlap
with the first.

SOME VOICES

ACT ONE

Scene 1

Mental hospital. Ray is standing by a window, a suitcase at his feet. Ives is nearby.

RAY. You shat on my window sill again, didn't you, Ives?
IVES. No.
RAY. Yes you did. You were drunk again and you couldn't be bothered —
IVES. No.
RAY. Couldn't be bothered going to the toilet so you —
IVES. Bring me your shit!
RAY. So you went to the window and dropped a turd out of your window and it landed on my window/sill.
IVES. Bring me your shit!
RAY. You did. It's the only explanation. *(Sniffs.)* Jesus, it's disgusting. *(Pause.)*
IVES. Are you a betting man?
RAY. Don't change the subject.
IVES. Like the horses, do you?
RAY. No I don't.
IVES. I used to like following around behind the horses and scooping up their shit.
RAY. Well, why don't you scoop/up your own?
IVES. It gave me something to do. Would you like to scoop up

my shit?

RAY. No.

IVES. Because I would like somebody to scoop up my shit. I am tired of scooping up other people's shit. Somebody should scoop up mine. That's why I leave it there.

RAY. Where d'you get the booze from, Ives?

IVES. I ought to rub your nose in it.

RAY. What?

IVES. Then you'd learn.

RAY. But it's yours. *(Ives puts a hand on the back of Ray's neck.)* Hey, Ives, Ives —

IVES. Do you know what they do to me?

RAY. What?

IVES. Everything. Worm balls in my mouth, fur balls in my mouth, tape recordings. They play the tape-recorded voices then they make me eat them.

RAY. Who does?

IVES. The loonies. They think that I'm loony too. They think that just because they like it, I like it. But I never liked it. Not in my food for God's sake — it's weird.

RAY. *(Beat.)* You could complain.

IVES. I am complaining. I am complaining to you and you're not even listening! *(Ives lets go of Ray. Pause. They look at each other.)*

RAY. I have to get going.

IVES. Where?

RAY. I'm going home. They're letting me out today.

IVES. No they're not.

RAY. They are, Ives.

IVES. They're just "letting you out." Just like that. Listen to me, you'll never survive out there. They know it, you know it. They been promising to let me out for years — years — and they haven't. Why? I don't know why.

RAY. They don't want me anymore, Ives. I'm not crazy enough.

IVES. I think you're crazy.

RAY. My time's up.

IVES. You're damn right your time's up.

RAY. My twenty-eight/days.

IVES. You're fucking right your time is up.

RAY. I'm/off.

IVES. Everybody's time is up. You only have to look at things out there. A world which drives people bananas. *(They look at each other. Ray takes out a piece of paper from his pocket and scrawls on it. Hands it to Ives who reads it and stuffs it in his mouth.)*

RAY. This is my brother's address. When you get out, look me up.

IVES. Twenty years I been here and never once has anyone offered to let me out. They made me eat shit. Not horse shit, real shit. I try to kill myself all the time and they stop me. They don't even care.

RAY. I'm going now.

IVES. They pretend to care — they profess to know how to be in the business of caring, which to me, sonny Jim, is no different to a butcher professing to know how to operate on the brain. I like it here. D'you understand? I love it! They won't/get rid of me.

RAY. Ives —

IVES. I belong here.

RAY. I'll see you round.

IVES. Probably yes probably birds of a feather and all that.

RAY. What?

IVES. Stick together.

RAY. Yeh. *(Ives clutches Ray's arm to stop him leaving.)*

IVES. You are marked, my friend. Do you understand me? Marked. *(Ray shakes his head, then nods it.)* For life. *(Pause.)*

RAY. See you, Ives.

IVES. Yes. *(Ray exits. Ives spits out the chewed-up piece of paper and catches it neatly in his hand.)*

Scene 2

Pete's flat. Morning. Pete is sitting at a kitchen table. Ray enters carrying a four-pack of beer and wearing a long old coat. He looks dishevelled, sleepless. They look at each other.

RAY. All right, Pete?

PETE. Yeh, I'm all right, you all right?

RAY. Yeh.

PETE. Where you been?

RAY. Oh, here and there.

PETE. Well, where? What's the matter — couldn't you sleep?

RAY. It's the room you gave me. The walls keep moving. It's shrinking.

PETE. What d'you mean shrinking? D'you have a nightmare?

RAY. I told you. It's getting smaller. It's a nice place, Pete, but it's definitely getting smaller.

PETE. Don't be daft. Smaller?

RAY. Where's the railway line? It was out there a minute ago.

PETE. *(Indicating beers.)* What's this?

RAY. D'you know I always like to know where the railway line is. Increases my sense of mobility.

PETE. Where'd you get 'em?

RAY. When does the train come?

PETE. Never mind when the train comes. Where d'you get those?

RAY. I found 'em.

PETE. Where did you find 'em?

RAY. An old man gave 'em to me.

PETE. What old man?

RAY. This old fella down by the canal. I don't know his name. I was watching the sunrise and there were lots of 'em all asleep.

PETE. What have you done?

RAY. It's all different now. Most of it's wasteland but on some they planted trees, plant boxes, little pathways.

10

PETE. And this fella just gave you his beers, just like that.

RAY. I was thirsty.

PETE. You didn't do anything, did you?

RAY. No. You want one? *(Pete pulls out a little phial of capsules from his pocket, shakes it.)*

PETE. Just hand 'em over. Have some breakfast and take one of these.

RAY. Is it just me or are things not the same colour anymore?

PETE. What d'you mean?

RAY. Green things. Green things aren't the same anymore, much more faded. Yellow's not the same anymore neither. And then there's the sun which is more ... white. Silver. It's either too bright or else not even there. And the sky.

PETE. Yeh, all right, Ray ...

RAY. Look at the sky, Pete. It's not the same. It's not even a proper blue anymore. Everything is different.

PETE. Ray. *(Pete pushes the phial towards Ray.)*

RAY. No thanks.

PETE. You have to, Ray, you know you do.

RAY. I'm not taking any more of that stuff. It addles my brain. Affects my judgment. *(Ray swigs on a beer and grins at Pete who holds out his hand for the beer.)*

PETE. Give it to me.

RAY. You know what those are, Pete?

PETE. I know what they are and I know you need 'em.

RAY. Horse tranquilizers. Major knockout drops.

PETE. Just take a couple.

RAY. Chlorpromazine. Like Lithium times ten. Or a smack on the head with a claw hammer, if you know what that's like. Hardly the elixir of life.

PETE. Listen —

RAY. I'm not listening.

PETE. If this stuff is going to keep you out of that place and stop you doing stupid things then you have to take 'em.

RAY. I don't want to.

PETE. That's not the point.

RAY. Well, what is the point? *(Pause.)* Have a beer with me, Pete. Let's sit down and talk about old times together.

PETE. We will, Ray, but first you have to do this. If this is going to work, you have to show willing.

RAY. Bollocks. Since when did willing get anyone anywhere? Eh? Eh, Pete? *(Pause.)* Thanks for picking me up yesterday.

PETE. It was a pleasure.

RAY. No, I mean it. When you came to the gate in the car and you got out and opened the boot for my bags it was … it was a good feeling. I mean I really had that, that leaving feeling. That feeling. That feeling of leaving … and arriving.

PETE. Good.

RAY. Remember all those times when you were either picking me up from somewhere or dropping me off? Taking me to the train. Meeting me off the coach. Remember the time I got lost in Scotland? Perth. Took myself off and got arseholed with the old men of Perth for three weeks.

PETE. Yeh, it was very clever.

RAY. And remember the time I got lost in Wales?

PETE. It's difficult to forget, Ray.

RAY. Tenby. Got myself arseholed with the young people of Tenby for three weeks. All rock shops and little pubs done up to look like barns and little barns done up to look like pubs.

PETE. Give us the beers, will you.

RAY. Leaving and arriving, Pete, that's what I was doing. Following a pattern established over years which —

PETE. The beers, Ray.

RAY. Because I'm a traveling man.

PETE. Ray.

RAY. Swap.

PETE. *(Confused.)* No, no swaps. I mean yes, swap. *(Pete holds out the pills, Ray holds out the beers, withdrawing them as Pete tries to grab them. Eventually Pete takes the four-pack and Ray takes the phial of pills. Pete stands, puts the beers out of reach.)*

RAY. Hey, Pete.

PETE. Yes, Ray.

RAY. I'm sorry I never made the wedding. *(Pause.)*

PETE. Well, you were tied up, weren't you.

RAY. I was going to be best man, wasn't I?

PETE. That's right, yeh.

RAY. I had a special little book and everything, all about what you do when you're a best man. The "etiquette" of being a best man.
PETE. And what do you do?
RAY. I dunno. Never read it. *(Pause.)* And, and I'm sorry I never made the divorce neither.
PETE. You didn't miss much.
RAY. Quick, wasn't it?
PETE. Like lightning.
RAY. I mean it, Pete. I am sorry. You been growing into an old fart without me.
PETE. Well, you disappeared. Things change when you disappear.
RAY. That's what I was saying, Pete. Everything's changed. Even the ... even the smells have changed.
PETE. Ray, listen ...
RAY. Except for one. One smell hasn't changed.
PETE. Ray, please ...
RAY. Remember when we was kids and we used to play in that old stream that runs underneath the brewery?
PETE. No.
RAY. Yes you do. We'd play with sticks having races. And sometimes the horses from the brewery came down and drank there. And sometimes Dad came down and drank there and all, when, he was working at the brewery. You remember that smell? That *mysterious* smell which we could never figure out what it was.
PETE. Horse shit.
RAY. Nah, it was a nice smell.
PETE. Ray, I've got to go to work.
RAY. I've figured out what it was. You want to know what it was, Pete? It was hops. *(Pause. They look at each other.)*
PETE. I'm expecting deliveries. You going to go and see that woman today? *(Ray opens the phial and tosses a capsule in the air, catches it in his mouth like a peanut.)*
RAY. What woman's that then?
PETE. The one they fixed you up with to sort out the thingie for your whatsit.
RAY. What whatsit?
PETE. After-sales service. *(Ray throws another capsule in the air, catches it in his mouth.)*

RAY. You want one?

PETE. No thanks.

RAY. It'll calm you down.

PETE. When are you going?

RAY. I'm not going.

PETE. You're going, Ray. *(Ray shakes his head.)* Have a bath and get ready.

RAY. I didn't ask to be fixed up with any woman.

PETE. You gotta do it, Ray. The people said you gotta do it. She'll fix you up with that fella. He's supposed to be very good.

RAY. What fella?

PETE. The fella they recommended for the whatsit.

RAY. *(Exasperated.)* What whatsit?!

PETE. *(Beat.)* Observation. He's gonna help you now you're out.

RAY. Help me?

PETE. Watch you. See you don't get in any/trouble.

RAY. He's not gonna help me.

PETE. Yes he/is, Ray.

RAY. They're not here to help, these people.

PETE. They're here to —

RAY. They're here to investigate the mind.

PETE. Yes. Your mind.

RAY. For fun.

PETE. No, not for fun!

RAY. Because they find it interesting. They do.

PETE. Ray! *(Pause. Pete pulls out a ten-pound note from his pocket and hands it to Ray.)*

RAY. What's this?

PETE. Money.

RAY. I thought we were going to talk.

PETE. Call me when you've finished. I'll give you directions, we'll talk.

RAY. I know where it is.

PETE. Corner of Askew and —

RAY. Yeh yeh yeh off you go. *(Pete hesitates, then puts on a jacket and exits. Pause. Ray tips his head back, spits the capsules one by one into the air and catches them in his hand. Puts them back in the bottle, stands, grabs the beers and exits.)*

14

Scene 3

The street. Dave is standing over Laura who has her back against a wall.

DAVE. I'm going to count to three, Laura.
LAURA. I don't know where it is!
DAVE. One.
LAURA. I swear, Dave, I haven't/even seen it.
DAVE. Two.
LAURA. Let go of/me.
DAVE. I'm warning you.
LAURA. What're you going to do?
DAVE. Three. I'm only going to ask you this once, Laura. Once. And then I swear I'm going to get angry.
LAURA. Then you're going to *get/*angry?
DAVE. Where is it?
LAURA. You're going to get *more/*angry.
DAVE. Now I'm losing my temper.
LAURA. I told you I lost it. *(Dave shoves her into the wall.)*
DAVE. Don't lie to me, tell me.
LAURA. I don't fuckin' know where it is.
DAVE. And mind your language. You got a mouth like a fuckin' sewer so you have.
LAURA. Leave me alone.
DAVE. You're a dirty slut. I don't need to waste my time with dirty sluts.
LAURA. Then leave me alone.
DAVE. I'll leave. I'll leave all right just as soon as you tell me what you did with it.
LAURA. Go on get.
DAVE. I am. I will. I'm gone. Believe me, boy. *(Pause.)*
LAURA. Good. Goodbye then.
DAVE. You probably sold it. Sold it to pay for a holiday with your

fuckin' fancy man. Is that what you did?

LAURA. What fancy man?

DAVE. Your little fancy man. I know you got one. To pay for your hacienda abroad with yer man there.

LAURA. What haci — I don't have a fancy man.

DAVE. They know I took it, Laura. Five-stone sapphire. In a cluster. Not a half hoop. A cluster! *(Beat.)* They know I been taking stuff to give it to you.

LAURA. Who?

DAVE. The boys, Laura.

LAURA. What "boys"? You live in a world of your own, so you do.

DAVE. The people I work for.

LAURA. But you don't work!

DAVE. Every job we've done I took stuff to give to you.

LAURA. I don't want it.

DAVE. I am trying to make you happy.

LAURA. By giving me a thick ear, I suppose.

DAVE. I love you, you stupid ugly cow.

LAURA. That's why you put my head through a third floor window last week.

DAVE. I am under pressure.

LAURA. That explains it then.

DAVE. They're coming after me. I am desperate.

LAURA. So next time you stick my head through a window and leave me to bleed to death I'll understand.

DAVE. Laura! *(Pause. Brushes her shoulder with his hand. Steps back.)* Just tell me who's it is. Come on, I can take it, if you tell me who's it is I promise I won't do anything. Not to you.

LAURA. It's yours, Dave.

DAVE. Tell me who you been getting friendly with.

LAURA. I haven't been getting friendly with anybody. I don't have any friends to be friendly with.

DAVE. So what am I?

LAURA. Don't be stupid.

DAVE. Don't call me stupid! I hate that.

LAURA. I haven't been outside that stinking flat in three months. I haven't even been out to sign on.

DAVE. I don't ask you to sign on still.

LAURA. I like to sign on. It makes me feel normal.

DAVE. I look after you.

LAURA. I don't want you looking after me. *(Pause.)*

DAVE. Give me the ring and we'll call it quits.

LAURA. Are you deaf?

DAVE. That's all I want. Or an arm or a leg or your guts! *(He slams her against the wall.)*

LAURA. I lost it!

DAVE. Where did you lose it?

LAURA. If I knew that it wouldn't be lost! *(Ray wanders on and watches, unseen.)* Down the sinkhole probably.

DAVE. "Probably"?

LAURA. I don't know.

DAVE. Well, "probably" I'll just smash your brains out with this brick, shall I? *(He stoops and picks up a loose brick, Laura screams.)* Eh? Maybe I'll finish it right here. How would you like that?

LAURA. Christ, help me somebody please!

DAVE. Shut up!

LAURA. Please!

DAVE. Oh, "please please"! D'you think they care? D'you think anybody really cares about you, Laura? Eh? *(He waves the brick about.)* I'll tell you something. I care about you, you don't care about me, so you know what suddenly — I don't care about you. *(Laura weeps.)*

RAY. Put the brick down. *(Dave looks around in wonder. Sees Ray.)*

DAVE. Fuck off.

RAY. No go on. You could take somebody's eye out with that thing.

DAVE. What?

RAY. It's dangerous.

DAVE. Is it now? And who the fuck are you?

RAY. Nobody.

DAVE. That's right, pal. Mister Fucking Nobody. You wanna have a go?

RAY. Not really. *(Dave looks at Ray, then Laura, then Ray again, then Laura.)*

DAVE. Wait a minute, wait a minute. *(To Laura.)* Who's this?

LAURA. I don't know. *(Dave heads for Ray with the brick.)* No, Dave, don't!

DAVE. I'll murder the pair of you! *(He flings the brick to the ground, marches up to Ray and grabs him by the shirt.)* You wanna fuck with me? Eh? You wanna rescue a poor cunt in distress? Think that'll earn you brownie points?

LAURA. Please, Dave, leave him alone.

DAVE. Why?

LAURA. I don't know why, I just think you should.

RAY. Yeh leave me alone.

DAVE. Where's the ring?

RAY. I don't know what you're talking about.

DAVE. Don't play games with me, cunt.

LAURA. He doesn't know for Christsake! He's just some nutter. *(To Ray.)* Go away. Go on.

DAVE. One word of advice, nutter. *(He headbutts Ray who instantly collapses.)* One little gem of wisdom. *(He kicks Ray in the guts.)* Don't ever, never fuck with another man's misery. *(To Laura.)* And if I ever catch you with another man I will kill you. Both of you. *(Dave exits leaving Laura frozen in shock. She snaps out of it and goes to Ray.)*

LAURA. O Jesus. Oh shit. What did you think you were doing? *(She helps him sit up. She touches his nose.)* Hello? Can you hear me? It's just a nosebleed is all. Can you feel your nose?

RAY. Ow!

LAURA. Sorry … *(Ray breathes hard, his breathing gets slower and slower, he cradles his ribs, his head hangs down, he seems to pass out.)* Jesus. I'll get you to a hospital.

RAY. No! No hospitals.

LAURA. You should see a doctor.

RAY. I hate doctors.

LAURA. *(At a loss.)* Come on then. *(She gets him to his feet and they hobble off.)*

Scene 4

Laura's bedsit. Ray is sitting on the bed. Laura is attending to his face.

RAY. It's all closed up. I can't see. I'm going blind. Was that your old man then?
LAURA. No.
RAY. Who is he then?
LAURA. Just a fella.
RAY. Just a dangerous bloody nutter. It's funny how you never see it coming. One minute you've got your feet on the ground and the next you're five feet away staring at the stars.
LAURA. You'll live.
RAY. He's not coming back, is he?
LAURA. I doubt it.
RAY. Very reassuring.
LAURA. You shouldn't have got involved.
RAY. He was going to kill you.
LAURA. I'll be the judge of that.
RAY. He was. He said so. *(Pause. Laura works.)* What was he doing that for anyway?
LAURA. That's my business.
RAY. He's lucky. He caught me when I wasn't looking.
LAURA. You'll know to mind your own business next time. *(Ray looks at her. Pause.)*
RAY. You're a bit of a hard nut, aren't you?
LAURA. What d'you mean?
RAY. You don't say much. I just saved your life, you saved mine. That's not to be sneezed at. I'm only being friendly. *(She works.)*
LAURA. That's what I'm afraid of.
RAY. Why? *(She sticks a sticking plaster over the bridge of his nose and steps back.)*
LAURA. Done.

RAY. Is that it?

LAURA. It'll do.

RAY. But my nose. I'm sure it's broken. Feels like his head's still up there.

LAURA. D'you want to go to the hospital or not?

RAY. All right.

LAURA. Can you stand? *(Ray stands shakily, pauses, then plonks back down clutching his ribs.)*

RAY. No.

LAURA. Try.

RAY. I just tried.

LAURA. Try harder. *(Ray tries again but can't.)*

RAY. It's sitting down that's done it. I shouldn't have sat down. It's like whatchmecallit, rigor mortis. I can't move my legs. I think I'm becoming a paraplegic maybe. *(He rubs his ribs. She puts her hands on her hips and weighs it up.)*

LAURA. Lift your shirt up.

RAY. What're you gonna do?

LAURA. I'm gonna check your ribs. You probably cracked one. *(He lifts up his T-shirt, she probes his ribs. He laughs involuntarily.)* What?

RAY. Cold. *(She probes again. He laughs again.)*

LAURA. D'you want me to help you or not?

RAY. Yeh.

LAURA. What's so friggin' funny then?

RAY. Nothing.

LAURA. Does this hurt?

RAY. No.

LAURA. This?

RAY. No.

LAURA. This?

RAY. N ... yeh. That does.

LAURA. This?

RAY. Up a bit ... up a bit more. Just there. Nice. *(Laura stops instantly.)*

LAURA. Look, if you're going to take the piss —

RAY. I'm not taking the piss.

LAURA. You can clear off right/now.

RAY. I'm not/I'm sorry.

20

LAURA. Friggin' cheek. *(She packs away the Band-aids, etc., in a small cabinet next to the bed, returns to Ray.)* What's the date today?
RAY. I dunno, why?
LAURA. When were you born?
RAY. August twenty-third. *(Beat.)* I'm a Leo.
LAURA. I'm seeing if you're concussed or not. How's your head feel?
RAY. Are you a nurse then?
LAURA. Don't be daft. I'm on the dole.
RAY. Well, for on the dole you make a great nurse. You know exactly what they do.
LAURA. I think I'd rather be on the dole. Pay's better.
RAY. No, but you're an expert. How do you know all this?
LAURA. Will you leave it. *(Beat.)*
RAY. What about this place then, is it yours?
LAURA. It's council, I rent it.
RAY. Does he live here too then, whatshisname?
LAURA. No, he doesn't — now do you think you can stand up?
RAY. Does he often do this sort of thing?
LAURA. Would you stop asking awkward questions.
RAY. Scrape you up against walls, fling bricks at people, it's not/nice.
LAURA. If you don't mind —
RAY. It's rude.
LAURA. I think it's time you were on your/way.
RAY. I've met his sort before. Got nothing better to do than go round whacking people and scaring the shit out of them. You see them walking around wired, angry, wound up ready to "ping." He probably practises. It's not the first time this has happened to me, you know. It's not the first time I've completely unwittingly pro-voked somebody. I just —
LAURA. If it's all the same to you —
RAY. Say the wrong thing or look at them the wrong way. People like this do not like to be looked at. It's instinctive. And it's like —
LAURA. If I could just get a word in/edgeways.
RAY. Pardon me for being so bold as to exchange a look in the street while I'm going about my business, pardon me for daring to speak to you because we do not speak to each other.
LAURA. I'm trying.

21

RAY. We just don't, not if we are complete strangers.
LAURA. Are you listening?
RAY. And it's like/what —
LAURA. Jesus Mary and Joseph!
RAY. Is your problem, pal? That's what I say. *(Pause.)*
LAURA. I have to go out. I don't want to be rude but I have an important appointment and so I have to go out.
RAY. Will I see you again?
LAURA. What kind of question's that? *(Pause. Ray gets up.)*
RAY. Makes sense to me.
LAURA. It would do, wouldn't it.
RAY. I'm sorry.
LAURA. So am I.
RAY. I'm going.
LAURA. Thank you.
RAY. Out the door.
LAURA. Thank you. *(Ray goes to the door.)*
RAY. I'm going out the door now.
LAURA. Thank you very much.
RAY. You're welcome. Are you going to be/all right?
LAURA. What? Yeh fine.
RAY. Fine then. *(Ray nods and exits.)*

Scene 5

The restaurant kitchen. Spanish guitar music plays. Pete is preparing two plates of food on a prep table. Ray watches, his face bandaged and eye black.

PETE. What the fuck happened?
RAY. Nothing happened.
PETE. What happened to your face?
RAY. Nothing happened to my face.
PETE. You shot your mouth off again, didn't you?

RAY. No.

PETE. Look at yourself, Ray. Christ. *(He examines Ray's face.)* This is a serious fuck-up. A serious one. I leave you alone five minutes and you're in trouble.

RAY. I'm not, Pete.

PETE. Yes, Ray, this is what I call trouble. What would you call it?

RAY. An accident.

PETE. You cannot afford to get into trouble. How can I impress this upon you? Because if you get into trouble I get into trouble. They'll come to me and they'll see this and they'll think what?

RAY. I dunno, what?

PETE. What do you think they'll think? They'll think you're in trouble that's what they'll think.

RAY. Maybe they'll think it was an/accident too.

PETE. Because the patient's brother, this person to whom we've entrusted him to, cannot be trusted. And nor can the patient. And so they put you away again.

RAY. *(Beat.)* It's quite a long/story.

PETE. I signed a form. I signed a bit of paper to get you out of that place. They said "Let's let him out, let's send him back to his family — even though he doesn't have a family anymore we'll find somebody," and they found me. I haven't seen you in years, I don't even know who you are anymore but, fuck, yes I'm here for you, Ray, and I put that in writing we go through a whole procedure and you don't … appear to give a shit.

RAY. I do give a/shit, Pete.

PETE. Don't tell me you walked into a door. Always walking into doors, weren't you? You'd vanish off the face of the earth and walk into a door somewhere. *(He speaks into an intercom on the wall.)* Two curly sausages for table five. *(He takes two plates to a serving hatch and puts them down.)* Got yourself arrested. Did you get arrested again?

RAY. I didn't get arrested, honestly.

PETE. You been beaten up — how else do you explain it? Why don't you just move into Hammersmith nick? You used to practically live there. Either that or me or Mum God rest her soul would be knocked up at all hours by the police 'cos they found you in some heap somewhere. You could be dead for all I know but all you think about is me me me ... *(Into intercom.)* Two curly sausages for table five what the hell's going on?

INTERCOM. Sorry, guv.

PETE. *(To Ray.)* Oh no, Pete, I'm all right, Jack-the-Lad I am. The wind changed and my face turned to pulp by itself.

RAY. Are you listening to me?

PETE. You can't live like that again, Ray, you're not up to it. You understand? *(Beat.)* It's what sent you screwy in the first place.

RAY. Nothing "sent me screwy."

PETE. Well, it hardly helped, did it?

RAY. Nothing "sent" me screwy, Pete. Nothing sent me.

PETE. I just don't understand it that's all I just ... don't understand.

RAY. Nobody understands it.

PETE. Why can't you just ... pull yourself together?

RAY. Pull myself together.

PETE. Something like that, yeh. *(Into intercom.)* Two curly sausages for —

INTERCOM. Curly sausage.

PETE. What?

INTERCOM. Curly sausage, yeh?

PETE. Yes curly —

INTERCOM. Not Polish?

PETE. No, not Polish —

INTERCOM. They want pizza —

PETE. Well, they can't have pizza —

INTERCOM. They changed their minds —

PETE. Tell 'em to make up their bloody minds.

RAY. How do I pull myself together, Pete? Is there a string or something that people just pull on every time they're in the shit?

PETE. You know what I mean.

RAY. Yes I do and I don't fucking like it.

PETE. *(Into intercom.)* The curly fucking sausages are getting curly fucking cold all right? *(To Ray.)* I employ imbeciles. It's cheaper but it has its drawbacks. *(He starts preparing another two plates.)* My kitchen hand is unwell, probably hungover. I'll sack him tomorrow.

RAY. Are you listening, Pete? *(They look at each other.)*

PETE. I'm sorry. You'll have to be patient with me, OK? You have to be patient with me I have to be patient with you. *(Long pause as Pete works.)*

RAY. You want a hand?

PETE. I'll be all right.

RAY. I could wash up the plates.

PETE. I've got an imbecile to do that.

RAY. Remember when Dad was here and I used to wash up? Chief dishwasher. It was his dream to have a place like this, wasn't it?

PETE. I dunno, was it?

RAY. It was. All that simple stuff he was doing, bacon, beans, omelette, he couldn't give it away, could he?

PETE. I still do that during the day.

RAY. And at night you do this. What is it? Italian? He liked Italian.

PETE. Mediterranean. Pizzas and curly sausage. Gourmet pizzas like with smoked salmon and artichoke hearts. Sour cream. The yuppies love it. *(Into intercom.)* Ask table seven if they're ready to order and interest them in the fish soup. *(Silence.)*

INTERCOM. Why?

PETE. Because I made fish soup today and if I don't get rid of it those fish'll start swimming again. *(To Ray.)* Sorry, where were we?

RAY. I could persuade 'em to have the soup.

PETE. Did you go and see that woman today?

RAY. Which woman?

PETE. Did you?

RAY. Yeh.

PETE. Because it's important, you know that.

RAY. I know that.

PETE. What did she say?

RAY. Said keep up the good work and come back in two weeks.

PETE. Two weeks, why two weeks?

RAY. Why not two weeks?

PETE. Was your face like that when you went to see her?

RAY. No, why?

PETE. Because if it was then she wouldn't have said that, would she? It'd be a different kettle of fish altogether. *(Into intercom.)* Pesto pizza pie for table four. *(Ray takes a plate to the hatch, puts it*

25

down.) What did happen to your face, Ray?

RAY. What's pesto pizza pie?

PETE. It's pesto and pizza … in a pie. Now just tell me/what —

RAY. In a pie?

PETE. Folded over like a pie, yeh, not many people do it …

RAY. I'm not surprised.

PETE. Ray, I haven't got all night.

RAY. *(Beat.)* I met this girl. Her old man was giving her a hard time — I mean a really hard time, Pete.

PETE. Oh, Ray, you didn't —

RAY. So I —

PETE. You stuck your nose in.

RAY. He was gonna brick her face. I told him to stop.

PETE. Oh, good plan, Ray, I'm sure that worked/a treat.

RAY. Quite freaked me at the/time.

PETE. Never get involved.

RAY. He was murdering her!

PETE. That's not your problem.

RAY. I didn't know what to do.

PETE. It's her problem. Every person has their own set of problems. Every person has a hand of cards they are dealt in this life. If somebody has a bad card you don't pick up their bad card.

RAY. Yeh, but murder, Pete —

PETE. You have your own bad cards.

RAY. Puts a different slant on things.

PETE. What are you doing tomorrow?

RAY. I dunno.

PETE. Yes you do know, Ray, because I just told you. Didn't I just tell you? You go and see the woman and you do what she tells you to do.

RAY. Yes, Pete.

PETE. And you do what I tell you to do.

RAY. Yes, Pete.

PETE. And you do what they told me to tell you to do. All right?

RAY. All right, Pete. But, Pete, I mean I just feel, Pete —

PETE. Ray Ray Ray — everybody feels. We all have feelings but we don't let them rule our lives. *(Beat.)* Are you hungry?

RAY. Starved.

PETE. Clear a space. *(Ray clears a space on the prep table. Pete goes to the service hatch.)*

RAY. But what am I gonna do with my time besides all that?

PETE. We'll cross that bridge when we come to it.

RAY. We have come to it.

PETE. Give it one more try. Eh? *(Beat.)* Have you ever had curly sausage before?

RAY. No.

PETE. Well, today is your lucky day. *(He plonks the plate down in front of Ray. Ray looks at it.)* And tomorrow will be my lucky day if you do what you're supposed to. Is that a deal?

RAY. It's a deal.

PETE. Eat your grub. *(Pete gets back to work. Ray stares at his plate.)*

RAY. Pete?

PETE. Yes?

RAY. What's curly sausage?

PETE. It's just sausage, Ray. It's just like straight sausage only it's curly.

RAY. *(Eating.)* Nice.

PETE. It's got spices in it, I dunno, herbs or something.

RAY. Tastes good.

PETE. Yeh?

RAY. Yeh.

PETE. Good.

Scene 6

The pub. A few days later. Laura is sitting at a table drinking and smoking a cigarette. Music blasts out. Ray wanders over with drink in hand.

RAY. Is … is anybody sitting there?

LAURA. Only if they're very small.

RAY. Can I sit there? *(Laura shrugs. Ray sits.)* All right? *(Pause.)* It's nice here. *(Beat.)* All my friends come here. *(Beat.)* They're not here at the moment.

LAURA. I like it.

RAY. It's a friendly place. I like the music they play. It's not old and it's not new. Very few pubs play this type of music nowadays. Are you Irish?

LAURA. What?

RAY. This is an Irish pub.

LAURA. I'm from Limerick.

RAY. Did you know that there is more drunkenness, suicide and madness amongst the Irish in London than any other race on earth?

LAURA. Is that so?

RAY. Yes, well, that's what they say because mostly you see they're away from their family and they're lonely probably and sometimes there's prejudice against 'em because of who they are and they can't get jobs and things but also mainly it's just loneliness. Have you got any family here or are you just on your own?

LAURA. I'm on my own.

RAY. Me too. I just got my brother. Me dad vanished some years ago but there's still my brother. My mother's dead. Cancer I believe. *(Pause.)* No cats, no dogs, no — what are they — little hairy things, in a cage ... I don't have any sisters. Do you have any sisters?

LAURA. Yeh, I've got a couple of sisters.

RAY. And do you like them?

LAURA. They're all right.

RAY. That's good because you have to be able to like your family. You have to be able to trust them but mainly you have to like them. And sometimes you just don't. Sometimes you don't trust anybody. Then again sometimes you form a vague attachment/to —

LAURA. I have no idea, no idea at all, what you are talking about. Can you see that? *(Pause.)*

RAY. Would you like a drink?

LAURA. Look, I'm sorry if it looked like I wanted you to sit down but in fact I really didn't. What I wanted was to be left alone. And I'm not just saying that, I mean it. I don't want to talk to anybody I don't want to see anybody I don't want to fight with anybody I don't want to drink with anybody smile at anybody play Let's Get To Know Each Other I just don't want to know. I'm in a bad mood.

RAY. Well, why'd you come here?

LAURA. Because … I'm in a bad mood. Why did you come here?

RAY. *(Beat.)* I was bored.

LAURA. You were bored so you thought you'd come and talk to me. *(Ray shrugs. Pause.)*

RAY. It's nice here. I live round here. My brother he runs a restaurant it's very busy, sometimes I help out.

LAURA. Really.

RAY. Yes, all the time. *(Beat.)* No, never. What happened to your face?

LAURA. What?

RAY. You/all right?

LAURA. Nothing happened.

RAY. That doesn't look like nothing to me. You got quite a shiner. And your lip's all cut. And your arm, look at your arm.

LAURA. I fell out of bed.

RAY. Ah, I'm always falling out of bed. Falling out of bed and walking into doors. You want to get some carpet in that place that way you won't bruise so easy. So so so did you get to your appointment? *(Laura looks at him then glances around the pub uneasily.)*

LAURA. Yes, thank you.

RAY. You must be up the spout then. Am I right?

LAURA. I beg your pardon?

RAY. Is it his then? That fella of yours?

LAURA. Yes it's his all his handiwork just like your nose. Any other/questions?

RAY. I'm surprised people still want to have babies. I find it fascinating. I mean they say you get a special glow and everything when you have a baby. Like a special … *(She gets up.)*

LAURA. I have to go.

RAY. Please stay, sit down don't get all — *(Ray gets up and puts a hand on her arm, she bats it away.)*

LAURA. Don't touch me!

RAY. Sorry!

LAURA. What is wrong with you?

RAY. I just want to get to know you a bit, what's wrong with that?

LAURA. You don't get to know somebody by just walking up to them in a pub and talking absolute friggin' rubbish to them for

29

half an hour.

RAY. What d'you want me to do?

LAURA. Are you simple or wha'?

RAY. I offered you a drink.

LAURA. That is not how it happens.

RAY. Well, how does it happen?

LAURA. I don't know!

RAY. You don't believe me, do you? I like you. I'm not being funny. I thought you liked me seeing as I saved your life and all. I can't do that every day you know, my brother ain't half got the hump. He don't believe me neither. *(Pause. Laura sighs and sits.)* You got nice eyes.

LAURA. I don't believe this.

RAY. Incredible blue like two swimming pools.

LAURA. You don't give up, do you?

RAY. Not really/no.

LAURA. I'm not going to sleep with you, you know.

RAY. What?

LAURA. I said … *(Lowers her voice.)* I'm not going to sleep with you. If that's what you're getting at.

RAY. I don't want you to sleep with me.

LAURA. It's out of the question.

RAY. I didn't ask you to sleep/with me.

LAURA. Because, because —

RAY. I don't want you to sleep/with me.

LAURA. I'm not sleeping with/anybody.

RAY. I don't want you/to.

LAURA. Just at the moment. Sleeping with people is not the answer to/anything.

RAY. I don't want you to sleep with me. *(Pause.)*

LAURA. And I'm not doing anything else either.

RAY. I don't want you to.

LAURA. Nothing, you understand? Nothing.

RAY. I don't want to. *(Pause. They look around sheepishly.)*

LAURA. Well, good. I'm glad we got that sorted/out.

RAY. Who said anything about sleeping with you?

LAURA. I just thought that might have been where things were heading.

30

RAY. 'Course not. *(Beat.)* I don't like sleeping anyway, it's boring. I've been asleep for too long.

LAURA. You know that's not what/I meant.

RAY. I can't sleep, at night my brother says, "Go to sleep," and I can't. I don't want to. I have nightmares. *(Pause.)*

LAURA. What d'you have nightmares about?

RAY. Strange things. Things are always the wrong colour or the wrong size. Things speaking to me. Like birds. I mean real birds that fly.

LAURA. What's so scary about that? I'd love to have nightmares about birds.

RAY. I scare easily. Well, I can't speak to them, can I? I'm not Doctor fuckin' Doolittle. *(Beat. She laughs a little.)* What about yours?

LAURA. Who said I get 'em?

RAY. You must do.

LAURA. Yeh, well … I wake up before anything really bad happens.

RAY. I know that sort and all. Awful.

LAURA. Yeh … awful. *(Pause.)* I'm/sorry I —

RAY. No, I'm/sorry.

LAURA. I didn't/mean to —

RAY. I just barged/in —

LAURA. No you —

RAY. I —

LAURA. I —

RAY. I'll get the drinks in.

LAURA. Get the drinks in, good idea.

RAY. A pint is it?

LAURA. Vodka. Double. *(Ray gets up hurriedly and goes to the bar. Laura smokes her cigarette. Pause. She fidgets. Ray returns and plonks a vodka orange and a beer down.)*

RAY. You shouldn't smoke and drink you know.

LAURA. There's a lot of things I shouldn't do.

RAY. But you still do 'em. Me too. I personally like to live as if I'm gonna die tomorrow.

LAURA. You might do.

RAY. Yeh, yes that's exactly it. That's exactly it. *(Pause.)* I'm Ray, by the way.

LAURA. Laura. *(Ray puts his hand out, they shake. Beat.)*
RAY. Can I have a feel?
LAURA. What?
RAY. Of your ... of the ... *(He indicates her belly.)*
LAURA. Of this? *(Ray nods. Ray puts his hand on her belly. Laura looks straight ahead. Ray puts his ear to her belly and listens. Laura looks around awkwardly.)*

Scene 7

Split scene. Ray is in a telephone box at the seaside, the sound of gulls overhead and waves. Laura strolls about outside throwing chips from a bag at the gulls. Pete is in his kitchen talking on the wall phone.

RAY. Pete.
PETE. Ray, is that you?
RAY. Pete, it's me.
PETE. Where are you?
RAY. Can you hear me?
PETE. I can hear you, Ray, where are you calling from? *(Ray turns to Laura, opens the door a crack.)*
RAY. Where are we?
LAURA. Southend.
RAY. Southend.
PETE. Southend? What are you doing in Southend?
RAY. I came to see the sea. Get away from it all.
PETE. Who are you with?
RAY. I met a girl.
PETE. What?
RAY. You know. A woman.
PETE. Don't fuck me about, Ray. I'm not kidding.
RAY. Nor am I. I met someone, a bird, a chick, a little tweetie-pie —
PETE. All right I get the message — who?

RAY. Her name's Laura.

PETE. Yeh and?

RAY. Lives up near the canal. Up Harlesden way. She's got her own place. It's a nice place, Pete.

PETE. How did you meet her?

RAY. You'd like her.

PETE. How did you meet this person, Ray?

RAY. Does it matter?

PETE. Yes it does matter.

RAY. I was just hanging around and she was hanging around and our paths just crossed.

PETE. You met her in the pub.

RAY. No/I swear.

PETE. You bloody fool, what on earth do you think you're doing?

RAY. Remember how I told you about the —

PETE. No more stories, Ray, I'm not/listening.

RAY. This bloke right —

PETE. Just come home.

RAY. And now he's —

PETE. Now. *(Pause.)*

RAY. You don't believe me, do you?

PETE. Oh, I believe you all right.

RAY. Do you want to speak to her? *(He leans out of the phone box. He wants to speak to you.)*

PETE. Ray, it's just fast work that's all.

RAY. It's a fast world, Pete. Sometimes things happen even too fast for even you to understand.

PETE. Oh, is that so? *(Beat.)* Listen, Ray, are you sure you didn't … black out or something?

RAY. Positive, Pete.

PETE. Because it wouldn't be the first time, would it?

RAY. No it wouldn't but I'm fine. I'm dandy in fact you could say I'm well chuffed. I like it here. It's like I'm in a movie, you know? All the people on the beach drink beers out of plastic cups and they play nineteen-fifties music.

PETE. You haven't been taking your medication, have you?

RAY. What's that?

PETE. Your pills. You left 'em here, you hardly touched 'em.

RAY. I forgot.

PETE. Jesus! *(Pause.)*

RAY. You still there, Pete?

PETE. When are you coming home?

RAY. I dunno. I might stay awhile, we been having a wicked/time.

PETE. Get on a train and come home. I got enough to deal with without you wandering off again. D'you want me to come and get you?

RAY. We'll be all right.

PETE. No, I'm coming to get you. Where are you?

RAY. What's that?

PETE. What's the name of the street? *(Ray makes static noises with his mouth, pulls a crisp wrapper from his pocket and ruffles it against the phone.)*

RAY. I can't hear you, Pete … it's breaking up … bad line … I … oh no.

PETE. Ray? Ray! Hello? *(Ray hangs up the phone. Pete listens for a moment then slams the phone down. Ray gets out of the phone box, lights a fag and looks around happily. Laura comes over, he gives her a fag and lights it up. Lights down slowly on Pete as he paces.)*

LAURA. What did he say?

RAY. Said stay as long as we like.

LAURA. Do you always have to ring him when you go somewhere?

RAY. He gets bored. I just ring to cheer him up.

LAURA. Are you sure he's OK about it? Sounds like you might have some explaining to do.

RAY. Nah, he just worries too much. Worries I might accidentally enjoy myself. He's like an old woman sometimes.

LAURA. Well, I think it must be nice to have somebody to worry about you like that.

RAY. It's a drag. Let's go on the pier.

LAURA. We been on the pier all day for goodness sake!

RAY. We'll go again. I like the pier. *(He grabs her hand and tows her away.)*

Scene 8

Tube station. Ives stands with shopping bags of belongings, drinking from a beer can and examining the note Ray gave him. Dave walks towards the tube dressed in a black suit and white shirt, top button done up, clean-shaven. He stops, turns and stares in the direction he's just come from, puffing on a cigarette.

IVES. Psst. *(Dave ignores him.)* Psst.

DAVE. Get lost. *(Dave continues searching.)*

IVES. The corner of Uxbridge and Askew.

DAVE. What about it?

IVES. Where is it?

DAVE. Have you seen a girl come out of that pub there?

IVES. Are you local?

DAVE. Have you? Red hair. Skinny.

IVES. It's important.

DAVE. Have you?

IVES. No. *(Dave checks his cuffs and collar and goes on staring.)* I'm lost.

DAVE. Everybody's lost. Now leave me alone before I break your fuckin' legs off. *(Beat.)*

IVES. That's a nice suit. *(Beat.)* Bespoke.

DAVE. Yeh yeh.

IVES. Nice.

DAVE. Yeh.

IVES. I had a suit once. *(Dave ignores him.)* Tailored. Five-inch vents. Three buttons. All the rage. You can respect a man in a suit and the ladies like it too.

Wear a Suit Today and Keep Heartache at Bay.

Once I Had a Secret Love and All Because I Wore a Suit.

DAVE. You're a bit old for that kind of talk, aren't you?

IVES. My old man swore by them.

DAVE. I look all right then?

IVES. Beautiful, man, beautiful.

DAVE. Yeh?

IVES. I had a friend and then he scarpered. *(Dave snatches the note off Ives, reads it and points.)*

DAVE. Straight ahead. Through the market.

IVES. Thank you. *(Ives moves to go, Dave stops him with a restraining arm.)*

DAVE. Then left.

IVES. Right.

DAVE. Then straight on. Then left. *(Ives moves again. Dave stops him.)* There's a kind of a … kink in the road. Watch for the kink. It'll be there for you somewhere.

IVES. Thank you.

DAVE. Any time.

IVES. Have a Guinness.

DAVE. G'way with yer.

IVES. You need it.

DAVE. I said no, OK? *(Pause.)* I'll go stark staring if I don't find her, you know that, don't you? *(Beat.)* D'you believe me? *(Beat. Ives drinks.)* I'll wind up like you. Fuck me. *(He digs into his pocket, pulls out a fiver, hands it to Ives.)* Go on get out of my sight. Get lost.

Scene 9

A field. Ray and Laura are on a blanket holding each other, not speaking. There is food and a bottle of wine and a four-pack beside them. Ray strokes Laura's cheek.

LAURA. You know we shouldn't be doing this. *(Beat.)* You could be some type of maniac. *(Beat.)* I could be some type of maniac. *(Beat.)* So why are we doing it?

RAY. We're just stupid I guess. *(They kiss.)* Wow.

LAURA. Yes, wow.

RAY. You're a good kisser.

LAURA. Yeh, well ...

RAY. Has anybody ever told you that?

LAURA. No. I mean yeh, so are you.

RAY. You got nice big lips. *(He puckers his mouth experimentally.)* Nice and firm. What shall we do now? *(She breaks away, folds her knees under her chin. Ray chews on a piece of straw.)*

LAURA. I didn't want this to happen, you know that, don't you?

RAY. Yeh.

LAURA. I've only just escaped from the last man I was with.

RAY. You can't keep escaping forever otherwise you'll run out of places to escape to.

LAURA. Depends on what you're escaping from. When I say escape I mean really escape. Like jump out of windows and dig tunnels type of escape that's what I'm talking about.

RAY. Mm.

LAURA. I mean, I thought I had escaped. This is me escaping. I escape all right but he just keeps coming back.

RAY. Persistent.

LAURA. Yes.

RAY. Why?

LAURA. He has to be with me the whole time or something. He goes mad if he's not with me. I go mad if he is.

RAY. Is that why he hit you?

LAURA. I don't know why he hit me.

RAY. Maybe he couldn't ... couldn't express himself or something.

LAURA. Maybe he just likes hitting people.

RAY. Maybe he was confused.

LAURA. I was confused but it's no excuse to —

RAY. Maybe he loved you so much ... that he just hit you.

LAURA. What on earth are you talking about? *(Pause.)*

RAY. No, maybe not. *(Beat.)* You must've liked him once.

LAURA. *(Sighs.)* He could be quite charming when he wanted to be so. Well ... not so much charming. Persuasive, I suppose.

RAY. What about when he hit you?

LAURA. Oh, he could be very persuasive then.

RAY. But you stayed with him.

LAURA. You get used to it after a while.

RAY. How can you get used to it?

LAURA. You don't expect it to … keep happening, I suppose. *(Beat.)* He was always after calling me a slut or a whore and then the next minute I was frigid. He'd accuse me of going with other men, then he'd say I'd never find another man who'd have me. *(Beat.)* If someone says something like that often enough, you find yourself believing it. It's a miracle the things you find yourself believing.

RAY. I know what you mean.

LAURA. I used to worry that I was going a bit mad because I still liked him. I'd get lonely without him and miss him because sometimes at night he could be something warm to get up against or something. When we'd been together his skin and his hands would always be warm … but when he came in after a night out he was cold, I mean his hands were cold his … knuckles. At first he could make things feel different. But then he couldn't. *(Pause.)*

RAY. Couldn't you go somewhere? Go home?

LAURA. They say I cause trouble.

RAY. I've heard that before and all.

LAURA. I don't need anyone telling me how to redeem my mistakes. *(Pause.)*

RAY. What d'you think would happen if we stayed here and didn't go back?

LAURA. Stayed here in this field?

RAY. Yeh.

LAURA. *(Shrugs.)* We'd die of starvation probably. *(Pause.)*

RAY. Kiss me. *(They kiss chastely. Beat. They kiss passionately and fall back on the rug. He kisses her neck and chest wildly, peppering her with kisses. She giggles.)*

LAURA. Euch, stop! *(He does.)* No keep going. Here … on my mouth. *(He kisses her on the mouth.)* Now squash me. On top. I want to feel your weight. *(He climbs on top.)*

RAY. Like this?

LAURA. Harder. Squeeze the breath out of me. *(He does so.)* Harder! *(He wriggles and laughs.)*

RAY. Why?

LAURA. Makes me feel safe. *(They lie like that for a moment. Ray*

kisses her neck, starts unbuttoning her dress.)
RAY.   You've got beautiful breasts, Laura. I want to suck them.
(They kiss, he puts his hand between her legs.)
LAURA. Bit higher ... down ... just there. *(Blackout.)*

ACT TWO

Scene 1

Pete's flat. Ray, Ives and Pete sit around the kitchen table. Ives and Ray drink beers.

IVES. *(Singing loudly.)* "I wish I was in London or some other seaport town I'll set myself on a steam boat and I'll sail the ocean round."

RAY. *(Simultaneously.)* De da de da de da ...

IVES. "While sailing round the ocean while sailing round the sea I'd dream of handsome Molly wherever she might be."

RAY. Join in Pete — "Wherever she might be."

IVES. "Her hair's as black as raven her eyes as black as coal her teeth are like the lilies ... "

RAY. *(Simultaneously.)* Da da de da ...

IVES. "That in the morning glow!"

PETE. I don't think I can take much more of this.

IVES. "And now you've gone and left me go on with who you please."

PETE. Enough!

IVES. "My poor heart is aching ... "

RAY. Ives, schtum. *(Pause.)*

PETE. So ... Ives, you were at Epsom with Ray?

IVES. Ah, yes, he's a good boy, lovely fella.

PETE. And ... how long have you been back in London?

RAY. He got out just after me.

IVES. Escaped.

RAY. Escaped just after me.

PETE. And you're living round here?

IVES. That's right. Underneath the arches. *(Singing loudly.)*

"Underneath the arches … "

RAY. Under the bridge. The flyover, isn't that right, Ives?

IVES. I, I, I, I, I, I'm not from round here no. I come from far away. A distant and very beautiful planet, the Planet Vega as a matter of fact.

PETE. I see. *(Pause.)* So … where is this planet Vega, then?

IVES. Don't patronise me. Do you think it's funny?

PETE. No.

IVES. *(To Ray.)* Does he?

RAY. I don't think so.

IVES. Do you?

RAY. Of course not.

IVES. It's not my fault. They came and got me, I didn't go to them. They took me away, took me to their leader. He told me all about you. Described you perfectly. *(To Pete.)* Especially you.

PETE. Really?

IVES. I was in the gasworks before that. Sixteen years in the gasworks and the whole fucking lot goes sky high. Explosion. I was there, I saw the missiles go up. High into the sky they went and on the ground a great flaming fireball. No safety precautions on account of the fact they wanted it to happen, you understand? They sent the missiles up as a signal. Why? To let them know I was ready. Why? Because they wanted to get rid of me. *(Pause.)*

PETE. Why would they want to get rid of you?

IVES. To save on early retirement. One month off early retirement I was. One month. Now look at me. There's not enough room any more. They want us all to go away!

PETE. I'm sure they don't.

IVES. What would you know about it? Look at you with your little baby-arsed face scrubbed clean and beautiful.

PETE. Ray —

IVES. I shall tell you what I think about the monied classes. They are the progenitors of beauty. The rich copulate with the beautiful and they breed. They breed more rich and beautiful. I do not like to be told that beauty is within because beauty is a commodity. I do not like to hear people say money is no obstacle because money is the obstacle. I don't need to be told as long as you have your health because you buy your health and so it is a question of as

41

long as you can afford it. I'm not stupid. I can think. I can see the people that pass me by. *(Pause.)*

PETE. Can I have a quiet word, Ray?

IVES. Hey you yes you! I'm talking to you. *(Pete and Ray get up and move a short distance away. Ives stands on his chair.)* THERE IS NO REVOLUTION! THERE NEVER WILL BE BECAUSE YOU ARE NOT THE REVOLUTIONARY TYPE!

PETE. Get him out of here.

IVES. NEVER IN THIS COUNTRY WILL THERE BE ANY-THING THAT SMACKS OF JUSTICE!

PETE. Enough is enough. This is my home.

RAY. Where's he gonna go?

PETE. Take him to a hostel or something. The Novotel anywhere. *(Pete pulls out a wad of notes from his pocket and hands Ray a couple.)*

IVES. You can't buy me.

RAY. It's not that easy, Pete.

IVES. You could make me an offer but I wouldn't think about it.

PETE. It is that easy. I want him out and I want you to deal with it. It's not too complicated even for you.

RAY. I said he could stay over. Stop here/for a while.

PETE. What?! *(Beat. They look at each other. Ives climbs down.)*

IVES. *(To Pete.)* I remember you.

PETE. Oh, Jesus …

IVES. You and this area and everybody here from when I was small …

PETE. *(Simultaneously, ignoring Ives.)* Are you insane? What are you trying to do to me?

IVES. My old mum she used to take us to the Bishop's Park as it was known then/when it was sunny …

PETE. I can't do it! I can't help! OK? Don't you understand?

IVES. The golden mile we trekked to the Bishop's Park where they had a lagoon with a little fake island/in the middle like a pot plant …

RAY. You'll get used to it, Pete.

PETE. It's blowing my circuits! He stinks, Ray. He won't shut up. It's like being in a … fuckin' lunatic asylum! *(Silence. Ives stands, drains his beer, pats his pockets, gathers up two more empty cans, shakes them and moves to the door.)*

IVES. ... I'm sorry.

RAY. Wait, Ives ... *(Ives exits. Pete sighs and sits at the table. Pause.)*

PETE. You know, Ray ... if you wanna piss your life away then fine but don't piss mine away too. You ... see what I'm saying? *(Pause. Ray sits at the table. Pete flicks up a can from the table, crushes it and throws it back.)* This is just what Dad used to do.

RAY. Is it now.

PETE. That's how he pissed his gaff away, pissed it all away drinking.

RAY. He was a drunk. That's what drunks do.

PETE. You never went through with him what I went through. Is that how you wanna end up? Is it? *(Pause. Pete pulls out the phial of pills from his pocket and plonks them on they table. Ray grabs them.)*

RAY. I been looking for those everywhere.

PETE. Do I have to stand over you morning and night every night for the rest of your life? *(Beat.)* For the rest of your life, Ray. *(Ray shrugs.)* And ... for the rest of my life. I mean how weird are things gonna get? You been out two weeks and you haven't done any of the things you're supposed to do. I'm keeping my end of the deal what about yours?

RAY. Don't talk to me about deals — I'm not doing any more deals.

PETE. You want me to force you, is that it?

RAY. How you gonna force me?

PETE. I don't know, Ray. I'm sure I'll think of something.

RAY. Drugs are bad for you, Pete. Everybody knows that.

PETE. Not these ones! Jesus.

RAY. They lead to worser things.

PETE. Oh, like what? Like ... him? Do you wanna end up under a bridge as well?

RAY. I'm weaning myself off 'em.

PETE. What?

RAY. Going for a more natural approach. I need a whatisit ... stable environment. Need to be around people I know and can trust and all that.

PETE. But you never are around, Ray, I never know where you are! Where do you go? Where have you ... Where have you been?

RAY. With Laura. I told you.

PETE. Oh, don't start that again.

RAY. "Don't start"? Don't start what again? *(Beat.)* You still don't believe me, do you? *(Beat.)* I'm tired of living here.

PETE. Why?

RAY. You got noisy neighbours. Every damn night I hear them revving up their fancy cars and popping champagne corks. What's the matter, Pete, you grown out of the Bush? You in a different bracket now so you don't notice things anymore?

PETE. What am I supposed to notice?

RAY. These ... arseholes. I've seen them trotting about in their tennis outfits with their dolly birds with the sunbed tans. I've seen them go where the sunbeds are and come back orange. They're probably all your customers. It's disgusting. What I need is a gun, a stun gun, that'd put a few holes in their party frocks. *(Pause.)*

PETE. Jesus, Ray, they're only —

RAY. Fuckers.

PETE. They're my neighbours.

RAY. It's doing my head in.

PETE. They're just people.

RAY. People do my head in. *(Pause.)*

PETE. You mean ... "doing your head in" or actually doing your head in?

RAY. I mean it gets on my tits.

PETE. Well, Ray, you don't have to live here. You don't have to do any of this. Nor do I. I mean ... *(Beat.)* Maybe you could get your own place. Bedsit or something. That's the idea, isn't it? Get you on your own two feet. *(Beat.)* I mean they can't expect you to stay here forever. Can they?

RAY. I'm going to Laura's.

PETE. Are you now.

RAY. Yeh.

PETE. Oh well, Jesus, why the hell not — you been going out with her for a whole two weeks. Good idea. *(Beat.)* You're serious, aren't you? There really is a Laura?

RAY. Yeh.

PETE. And that's where you been staying?

RAY. What's wrong with that?

PETE. *(Beat.)* OK, well then, maybe we should do something.

(Beat.) Talk to them about it. *(Beat.)* We'll go in there and tell 'em there's a change in plan. Fuck their plan, it isn't working, there's a new one. Why not?

RAY. I already have.

PETE. What?

RAY. She said it's a good idea too.

PETE. *(Laughs.)* Just like that. Just like that she said, "Go ahead, shack up with this bird, enjoy yourself."

RAY. That's right, more or less exactly what she said.

PETE. You actually went to see her?

RAY. Yeh, she had a ... mole on her lip.

PETE. *(Sotto voce.)* I don't believe it ... *(Pause.)*

RAY. It's going to be all right, Pete.

PETE. Come on, Ray, this is stupid. It's stupid!

RAY. Don't worry about it.

PETE. I can't help worrying about it.

RAY. You have a business to run.

PETE. I know, yes I know that —

RAY. And there's nothing you can do anyway. *(They look at each other.)*

Scene 2

Laura's flat. Morning. The telephone is ringing. Ray and Laura are sitting up in bed. Ray is smoking a cigarette. After a while he leans over, picks up the receiver and hangs it up. Pause. Laura takes Ray's hand and places it on her belly.

LAURA. Feel. *(She plonks Ray's hand on her belly.)* He'll be wanting to come out soon enough. He'll be walking about and talking and expecting to learn things. What am I going to teach him? *(Pause.)*

RAY. I never thought of it like that.

LAURA. I dreamt that I'd already had it. It was tiny. About the size of my thumb and it was blue. Blue and white and red and made of plastic. With ... some kind of light on it and the light said whether it was still alive. I carried it round on the bus with me waiting to tell somebody but I was too afraid. I worked out that the light meant how warm it was and I was afraid I didn't have enough warmth. I went into a pub and had a drink and when I came out ... the light had gone out. And it was dead. I felt so ashamed. *(Pause.)*

RAY. Which pub?

LAURA. Ray!

RAY. What? *(She hits him with a pillow.)*

LAURA. You're supposed to listen to me!

RAY. *(Laughing.)* Am I?

LAURA. Yes! Look at you — far away in your own little world, dreaming your dreams.

RAY. I know, I —

LAURA. The lights are on but there's nobody within miles!

RAY. *(Delighted laughter.)* That's right. Not even, not even squatters.

LAURA. I'm serious.

RAY. Me too. Because ... you are more screwy than me. Sometimes. You are. You're off your head. You've flipped your lid. You've popped your hatch ... *(She hits him with the pillow.)*

LAURA. Shut up.

RAY. You've popped your cork, you're off your stick, you've lost your conkers, marbles ... *(She hits him with the pillow.)*

LAURA. Shut up, you fool!

RAY. *(Laughing.)* You've burnt the soup. You've shredded the screw. You've lost the soap. You, you ...

LAURA. Come here. *(He puckers his lips and moves his face closer. Laura smacks him in the face.)*

RAY. *(Delighted.)* Beautiful. Do it again. *(She grabs him by the ears, makes to kiss him and blows a raspberry into his lips.)* I like it. I really do, Laura. It blows me away. *(Pause.)* I just ... I just want to put my body against your body. That's all I want. I like your body. I like the curves. I like the bumps and the ... mounds. And what's inside. Whatever it is that ... powers you, Laura, I like it. So warm. So warm.

LAURA. Are you trying to tell me something?

RAY. I just did. *(They look at each other. The phone rings.)* Don't answer it. *(Beat.)* You don't like answering the phone, do you? Why not? *(Ray picks up the phone. Laura snatches it.)*

LAURA. Hello … hello? *(Pause.)* No thanks. *(Pause.)* Because I don't want to that's why. No … Because I don't. And I don't want to go to the pub … I don't want to play pool … I don't want to play darts either. *(Pause.)* No!

RAY. Hang up.

LAURA. Don't you call me that.

RAY. Hang up the phone.

LAURA. What? That's not a man's voice, I just coughed … So when I cough I sound like a man. *(Ray grabs at the phone. Laura hangs on and speaks into the phone.)* Bastard. *(She slams the phone down. Pause.)* He wants me to meet him. *(Beat.)* He says I have to meet him. *(Beat.)* He says if I don't meet him he's gonna break my legs.

RAY. What're you gonna do?

LAURA. What do you think? *(Pause. Laura gets out of bed and pulls on jeans and a jumper. Ray gets up and searches for his clothes.)*

RAY. He'll break your legs anyway. It doesn't make any difference to him. He's a/psychopath.

LAURA. If I don't go and he comes round here he'll break your legs too!

RAY. *(Beat.)* You think so?

LAURA. I know so. *(He hesitates, then pulls on a pair of pants and pulls a jumper over his head and hops about with the pants half up and the jumper half on.)*

RAY. You need looking after. He needs dealing with. That's where I come into it.

LAURA. Ray, no.

RAY. What if something happens? *(Laura goes to the bed, pulls from under the pillow a hammer. She picks up her bag, puts the hammer in the bag.)*

LAURA. Nothing is going to happen.

RAY. What the fuck's that?

LAURA. What? This hammer?

RAY. Yeh.

LAURA. It's a hammer.

RAY. You sleep with a hammer?

LAURA. I lost my baseball bat.

RAY. I don't think that's wise, Laura. Nine times out of ten if you pull a hammer on somebody they'll use it on you. *(Beat.)* What if he tries to make friends with you or something? Tries to … worm his way back into your affections.

LAURA. Then it'd be a miracle. *(They look at each other. Laura exits.)*

Scene 3

The river. Dave and Laura sit on a bench by the water. Dave is wearing his suit, which is a little shabbier now, top button undone etc. He drinks from a bottle in a brown paper bag and is drunk.

DAVE. I looked at myself in the mirror and I said to myself, I said, "I am a man. A man who can look after his self but not a happy man. Not a complete man." And then I asked myself, "What is a man without a woman? What is he?" No job, no money, no faith will ever lead him to anything by his self. But with a woman …

LAURA. Isn't the sight of the empty bridge the most beautiful thing you ever seen? *(Pause. Dave drinks.)*

DAVE. I was a miserable man, Laura. I saw the darkness stare me in the face. Sometimes I'd come over cloudy. All strangely cloudy and I'd ask myself, "Why?" Why is the question. And then I'd put it to myself *hypothetically* what would we have done if we were married? And … and then I tell myself, "We would've worked at it."

LAURA. But we weren't married.

DAVE. Yes, but what if we were? And we did this to ourselves what we're doing now? Divorce? *(Singing vaguely.)* D. I. V. O. R. C. E. King Henry the Eighth — he was not a happy man. Why? Because he didn't work at it. And why? Because … he had no son.

LAURA. But we *weren't married*.

DAVE. And why is that? Because … because … I don't know why. I'm no philosopher, Laura, but thinking aside, you light my

48

wick. Eh? You do it for me. (*Long pause. He looks at her.*) I don't want to be with another woman in the whole of Shepherd's Bush. I love you, Laura.

LAURA. But that's what you say every time.

DAVE. I mean it this time.

LAURA. That's what you say every time too.

DAVE. And I mean it every time.

LAURA. Well, maybe you don't mean it enough. (*Pause.*)

DAVE. You know you say no to me, Laura, you say no to me every time, but I know and you know, you mean yes.

LAURA. I have to go. (*She makes a move to go, he puts a hand on her shoulder.*)

DAVE. I'm trying to say I'm sorry.

LAURA. You can't say you're sorry. There are things you can't apologise for, Dave. There are things you must not do and if you do 'em ... then you can't apologise.

DAVE. I never meant to hurt you.

LAURA. Why did you?

DAVE. I was under pressure ...

LAURA. I was under pressure!

DAVE. There's a ... force inside of me and I can't control it. I don't know what it is.

LAURA. Thirteen pints of Guinness is most of it.

DAVE. I'd do anything for you, Laura. I'd go on my knees for you. I'd do a ten stretch in the Scrubs, knock off Willy Hill's, blow up the Houses of fuckin' Parliament. I'm serious. (*Pause.*) I want to be a daddy. (*Silence.*) I said —

LAURA. I heard.

DAVE. But you —

LAURA. I heard and I don't —

DAVE. Can't comprehend.

LAURA. No, I —

DAVE. You're a bit surprised.

LAURA. No, Dave —

DAVE. You —

LAURA. I don't believe my fuckin' ears is all. (*Pause.*)

DAVE. Think about it, Laura, eh? Will you do that?

LAURA. He'll be born from the bottle but he won't be brought up by it.

DAVE. I'll stop tomorrow.

LAURA. You can't stop tomorrow.

DAVE. I'm trying to do what's right.

LAURA. You don't know what's right.

DAVE. And bringing a helpless kiddie into the world to live off slops and benefits is?

LAURA. We'll survive.

DAVE. What are you going to tell him when he wants his da'? When he wants a father's hand to hold in the night?

LAURA. It's not about that.

DAVE. It's about blood, Laura. Our blood and his blood. You know that's all that matters. *(He produces a ring from his pocket, holds it up.)* I found this. You didn't lose it, Laura … I did. *(Pause. Laura regards him. He holds it out to her insistently but she refuses to touch it.)*

LAURA. You mean you lied.

DAVE. We could be a real family, Laura.

LAURA. Just leave me alone. I curse the day I met you. *(Laura gets up and walks away.)*

DAVE. And the day I met you was the day the Angel of Joy came down from the heavens, so it was. *(Dave drinks.)*

Scene 4

Pete's flat. Pete, Ray and Laura are at the table, the remains of lunch, a few cans and a couple of bottles of wine spread in front of Ray.

RAY. Just lying around. Sleeping, eating, shopping. All the simple/things.

LAURA. Shopping? Don't talk to me about shopping. I've never seen anybody so afraid of a supermarket in my/life.

RAY. Drinking, shagging —

50

LAURA. He's allergic to it, I think.

RAY. It's not the supermarket, Laura, it's the people. All those people bickering over which brand to buy, whether to buy meat or fish, is it cheaper in the market?

LAURA. Everybody has to eat — tell him he has to eat, Pete.

PETE. You have to eat, Ray.

RAY. Haven't they got anything better to do except drag their fat arses around with their fat husbands and their screeching kids? If I was a mother I'd leave 'em there — let 'em gorge themselves to death on fucking Mars Bars.

LAURA. He's banned shopping entirely.

RAY. There's a lot of things I've banned entirely.

LAURA. Won't be seen dead on a bus.

PETE. I hate buses. People on buses are fools.

LAURA. Tubes ...

RAY. Why there's not more homicides on the tube I can't understand.

LAURA. Completely antisocial. I thought/I was.

RAY. I just mind my own business, Laura.

LAURA. You do not mind your own business. You don't.

RAY. I need a drink. *(Ray reaches for a bottle and refills his glass. Drinks.)*

PETE. I think you've had enough.

RAY. Enough? No, that's just where you're wrong, Pete old boy — I haven't had nearly enough.

PETE. Come on, Ray. You've had your fun. *(Pete pulls the phial of pills from his pocket. Puts it on the table. Ray looks at it. Pause.)*

RAY. I haven't even started yet.

PETE. I won't take no for an answer.

RAY. That's the only reason you invited me, isn't it? You didn't want to meet her at all. You just got me round here to take me fuckin' dose.

PETE. Now don't make a scene.

RAY. "Don't make a" ... a what? Listen to his Lordship. I am sorry, Pete old fruit —

PETE. Ray, come on.

RAY. For getting in ... for getting on your nerves and ruining your special ... lunch-time thingie. *(He laughs. Pause.)*

51

LAURA. What are they?

RAY. I have heart trouble.

PETE. They're just pills he's taking.

LAURA. What're they for?

PETE. They're just —

RAY. They're to stop me getting upset when my big fucking/bastard brother —

PETE. Didn't he —

RAY. Gets on my big ... fucking ... on my tits that's what they're for. *(Pause.)*

PETE. Didn't you ... tell her about ...

RAY. About what, Pete?

PETE. About ...

RAY. Oh, about " ... "

PETE. Yeh.

RAY. No. *(Pause.)*

PETE. Ray has to take this medication this special medication because sometimes he gets depressed.

RAY. I get depressed.

PETE. Doesn't sleep too well sometimes.

RAY. Can't sleep that's true.

PETE. Sometimes he *only* sleeps.

RAY. I do stupid things.

PETE. Yes he, stupid things, he —

RAY. I —

PETE. He —

RAY. I mean really stupid. Schizo.

PETE. Yeh he ... schizo. *(Beat.)* That's what he does. *(Pause.)*

LAURA. Oh.

RAY. I mean I don't eat babies or anything like that.

PETE. No no no no no. No, he doesn't do that. *(Silence. To Laura.)* So when's it due?

LAURA. What?

PETE. The ...

LAURA. Oh, the ... December. Yeh December.

PETE. December.

LAURA. December, yes.

PETE. Just in time for Christmas.

RAY. Now we're talking about babies.

PETE. Is it kicking yet?

LAURA. No.

RAY. Now we're — if he kicks you —

PETE. Ray, that's/enough.

RAY. Kick him back. Give yourself a ... do-it-yourself abortion. Save yourself the agony. *(Pause.)*

PETE. Oh, Jesus.

RAY. I mean it. You should see the father.

LAURA. I beg your pardon?

RAY. Christ knows what's gonna hatch. *(Laura smacks him in the face and stands.)*

PETE. No, Laura, please.

LAURA. That's the most horrible thing you could say to me. That's the most ... that ...

RAY. What?

PETE. Jesus, Ray, can't you —

LAURA. Don't you get it? Don't you understand anything? I want this baby, Ray. I want it. I'm worried about it and I know I probably can't look after it properly but I want it. More than, more than anything ... *(She sits down. Pause.)*

RAY. I don't know why.

PETE. Ray —

LAURA. Because it would be mine ... mine forever and it wouldn't hurt me and it wouldn't upset me and it would love me and it would trust me and I would ... I would trust ... it ...

RAY. But babies are horrible, Laura. They stink and cry and piss and poo everywhere. Everybody knows that.

PETE. Ray, for Christsake! *(Laura gets up and starts clearing plates.)* It's all right I'll do that. *(Laura ignores him.)* Talk sense, Ray, if you can.

RAY. I'm trying, Pete, I'm honestly trying to.

PETE. Shh ... just don't say another word. You push people too far.

LAURA. It's all right, Pete, I'm sorry.

RAY. No, Pete, no I don't because you push me too far. You two ... you don't even know each other. What the fuck do you care about each other? You pretend that's all ... you pretend to care that she ... you pretend to have this concern that I ... you're just ...

You know what you are? You're ... selfish. And ... responsible. Incredibly responsible. *(Pause. To Laura.)* Not you, him.

LAURA. I think we should be going.

RAY. I'm going to piss. *(Ray gets up; Laura stops him.)*

LAURA. Come now if you're coming. You can piss at my place. *(To Pete.)* Thanks for the —

PETE. Any time —

RAY. Why would I wanna piss at your place? Sit around at your place waiting for Joe Bugner to come home and —

LAURA. That's enough!

RAY. Give us both another beating?

LAURA. I'll give you a beating if you/don't —

RAY. 'Cos that's what's gonna happen. Oh yes, I can tell, he's gonna come around and he's gonna kill us both dead in our bed. And then I am going to kill him and then they'll put me away for good. They'll never let me go cos I'll be in Broadmoor or something with Jack The Fucking Yorkshire Ripper do you want that do you think that's reasonable? Eh? Well, do you? *(Laura just looks at him, can't speak. She grabs her bag and exits. Long pause.)* She's got a hammer in that bag. She has. She's more barmy than me.

PETE. Are you gonna tell me what that was about?

RAY. No. *(Pause.)*

PETE. Why did you do that? Why do you have to ... *(He breaks off. Pause.)*

RAY. I'm drunk, Pete.

PETE. Well, why do you have to drink like that?

RAY. I get depressed.

PETE. But, Ray, you drink when you're depressed, you drink when you're happy, when you're bored, it doesn't help.

RAY. It does.

PETE. She's having a baby, man. There's some fella out there who's having a baby *with* her. I mean a married woman's one thing but up the spout's a whole new kettle of fish, Ray.

RAY. She's not married.

PETE. Does she want to be?

RAY. She just —

PETE. How well do you know her? How well does she know you? Have you even considered —

RAY. No I haven't considered.

PETE. The implications? *(Beat.)* I mean I'm coming to the end of my rope here. I'm right at the end. This is just … you're just … this is just hanging on a hair here. I can't fucking do it anymore.

RAY. *(Beat.)* Well, that's life, isn't it?

PETE. I mean … "Selfish"? "Responsible"? *(Pause.)* Maybe you're right. Maybe that's where I've gone wrong … Maybe my wife left me because I was this selfish cunt who wore a pinny and tossed salads all day for other people. Maybe I should never have tried to save Dad or his greasy old gaff or his doomed fuckin' life 'cos that would have just been responsible, I dunno …

RAY. You bought him out, Pete. It was the one thing he loved and you took it off of him for a handful of notes.

PETE. Jesus, Ray — I just … had this weird idea that the thing to do was to go to work and do an honest day and pay a few bills and, look after your family and … I mean … he couldn't do it. I mean sooner or later somebody's gotta … make a stand. I don't see what's wrong with that. *(Pause.)*

RAY. Well, it's a bit boring, innit, Pete …

PETE. You're not the only one going out of your mind. You know I'd jack this in tomorrow if I had half a chance. Get on the old rock'n'roll and piss off to the seaside with some little bird I met in the pub … I'd love to.

RAY. Why don't you?

PETE. Because I am obliged, Ray … to do this thing for you. It is what I have to do. You understand? The measure of a man (no, listen to me.) in this life is whether he can do … what he thinks he has to do. *(Pause.)* I mean … why do you say these things to people?

RAY. I don't know.

PETE. Is it you or is it the … sooner or later you're gonna have to make up your mind. *(Beat.)* Tell me. *(Beat.)* Please.

RAY. *(Suddenly laughing.)* You're breaking my heart.

PETE. What?

RAY. Who fucking cares? *(Ray continues to laugh and swigs on a bottle.)*

PETE. Get out.

RAY. What?

PETE. It's none of my business. It isn't and I cannot make it my

55

business no matter who says I should. I have my own business. *(Ray gets up and starts to go.)* I mean it I've had enough. You just —
RAY. OK.
PETE. Get. *(Ray exits.)*

Scene 5

Wasteland. Ives stands alone. Ray is huddled under old blankets, paper and his coat at the foot of a nearby wall.

IVES. There will be a zone for the lost and the loveless and the godless and the demented and the dead and the half-dead and the damned and all of those who no longer live in the light, who only live in the dark. And that zone will be a terrifying place, and that zone will be the only place, and that zone will be all around you. You will not be able to walk in the streets that you walked in tonight. You will not be able to go where you are going without seeing the zone, or some small part of it, or one of the beasts that live in the zone, or the beast that made the zone. Believe me. There is nowhere. Nowhere you can go to hide from it. Nothing you can do to eradicate it. You will never be able to clean it. You will never sweep it under the rug. The city will become that zone. You will all be of that zone. The zone that is the, turd that you can never polish. You are all flies. Flies on the fleck of shit that is this world.
RAY. Ives …
IVES. Your world. The new world. Your new home. It will be built by contractors and its management put out to tender. There will be no crèche, no fire escape, no stairs and it will stink of piss and disease just like every other place before it.
RAY. I'm trying to sleep.
IVES. Don't deny it. You can't argue with me. You can't tell me, you don't believe me, when I tell you, that you are going to burn in hell. I am going to burn in hell, the blossoms on the trees are going to burn in hell.

RAY. Have you made any money yet?

IVES. I know what I am talking about. I am the authority on this kind of thing. I am the only authority you want to listen to and if you don't believe me you can jam it up your arses and whistle because I have had enough. I am disgusted with you, with me, with everything and I am tired of telling you. *(Ray gets to his feet and puts his hands over his ears.)*

RAY. Shut up, I'm not listening.

IVES. I am disgusted with the sky. With the water. The trees bore the daylights out of me ...

RAY. No, stop! *(Ives staggers and collapses.)*

IVES. I know you don't like it. I don't like it. But I told you this would happen. I warned you. I'm trying to be reasonable about it ... *(Silence.)*

RAY. Ives ... Ives old boy. Don't die on me now.

IVES. Nightmares ... nightmares happen ...

RAY. Come on, Ives ... we'll go somewhere warm. I'll take you to a launderette.

IVES. I brought home the bacon once ... I did ... to my wife. *(Pause.)* From the Isle of Skye, she was. *(He's dead. Ray just stares at him, unable to shift his gaze. He looks around suddenly, distracted by a noise.)*

RAY. What d'you mean? *(Pause.)* What's wrong with the launderette? He was cold. *(Pause.)* No, because there's nothing wrong with me. *(Ray stares straight ahead, listening.)*

Scene 6

Laura's bedsit. Early morning. Laura, dressed in leggings and a sweater, is sitting on the end of the bed, staring into space. There is a knock at the door. Laura doesn't move. Another knock and she goes to it.

LAURA. Who is it?

RAY. *(Offstage.)* It's me. *(Laura hesitates then goes to the door, thinks better of it and backs up, nervous.)* Laura? *(Pause. Another knock.)* Are you all right?

LAURA. What do you want?

RAY. I want to come in.

LAURA. It's seven o'clock in the morning.

RAY. I have to talk to you. I have something to tell you.

LAURA. What is it, Ray?

RAY. Let me in and I'll tell you. *(She opens the door a crack.)* I missed you.

LAURA. Ray, you have to go.

RAY. Did you miss me?

LAURA. Not really, no.

RAY. I was worried about you.

LAURA. Were you now.

RAY. Yes. I can't stop thinking about you. I keep thinking about when we were in the field in the countryside. The grass was like hay and the yellow sun shone and shone … we were making hay while the sun shone, weren't we, Laura?

LAURA. Yeh, that's right — *(He brushes past into the room.)*

RAY. We were making hay while the sun shone, weren't we?

LAURA. What do you want?

RAY. But it was more than that, wasn't it?

LAURA. Ray, I'm begging you —

RAY. It was more than that.

LAURA. I'm not well.

RAY. What's wrong with you? Are you sick?

LAURA. I'm just tired.

RAY. How sick?

LAURA. It's too late.

RAY. You looked so beautiful …

LAURA. Keep away.

RAY. We kissed and you smelt of blossom. *(Dave enters in trousers but no shirt, a towel slung over his shoulder. Stands at the door unseen by Ray.)* You understand me, Laura.

LAURA. No I don't! Shut up!

RAY. Yes you do and I understand you and there is nothing else. There is nothing else is there Laura? Nothing that matters … I know I'm in trouble now. I can tell things are going wrong — but I just ... I, I, I, I love you, Laura. *(Dave laughs. Ray glances over his shoulder and sees Dave. Turns around to face him. Pause.)*

DAVE. *(Mimicking.)* "I, I, l-l-love you Laura." *(Beat.)* You gonna introduce us? *(Pause.)*

LAURA. *(To Ray.)* I'll be seeing you.

DAVE. Fine way to speak to a lady. Is everything all right then, Laura?

LAURA. It's fine.

DAVE. Who's yer man then?

LAURA. Nobody.

DAVE. I'll tell you what, he looks familiar.

LAURA. He's going. *(Dave scrutinises Ray.)*

DAVE. Maybe it's the pub. You drink in the Adelaide there? I seen a few fellows like you in the Adelaide. Queer fellows. D'you think that's where our paths crossed? Doesn't say much, does he?

LAURA. Ray ...

DAVE. He's got a name then. Nice name. Are you gonna tell me what's going on?

LAURA. He's going, Dave.

DAVE. Are you gonna tell me what's going on or not?

RAY. Leave, leave her alone please.

DAVE. *(Mimicking.)* "L-leave her alone please. L-leave her a-lone p-please." *(Laughs.)* He can talk then yer man? Not very well but it's a start.

LAURA. Ray, go.

RAY. What ... what have you done?

LAURA. Nothing, just —

RAY. What have you done!

LAURA. I don't know I can't tell you! *(Ray just stares at her then tries to leave. Dave bars his way.)*

DAVE. No no no no no no no. No no no no no no no. Oh no. I don't think you should do that. I mean you can if you want — if you're the type of man who does something just because his lady friend gets her keks in a twist —

LAURA. Don't start, Dave.

RAY. Get, get out my way please.

DAVE. I beg your pardon?

59

RAY. Get out my way thank you. Please I would like you to get out of my —

DAVE. SHE LOVES *ME* — YOU UNDERSTAND? SHE. LOVES ME.

LAURA. I don't, I don't!

DAVE. Cunt. Shut up!

LAURA. Please!

DAVE. ON YOUR KNEES! *(To Ray:)* What are you looking at? *(He grabs Ray by the shirt, backs him up a few paces very fast against the bed and flings him across it, Ray lands on the floor beside the bed. Dave to Laura:)* Knees! *(Laura, panicked, gets on her knees. Dave to Ray:)* Watch.

LAURA. No ... no ... no ... *(Dave undoes his belt, gets behind Laura and ties her hands behind her back. Ray watches horrified. Dave wrestles with the belt, pushes Laura's head down roughly, Laura struggles.)*

DAVE. Why him, Laura? Eh?

LAURA. *(Struggling.)* Why not him? *(Dave pulls Laura's leggings down, tying up her legs.)*

DAVE. Cos he's a fucking eejit that's why. I've seen him, mincing about like a fairy with his brother, talking to his self, I've seen him, everybody has. Mad as a fucking whippet. *(To Ray.)* I know you. I know who you are. Did you think I didn't recognise you?

LAURA. Please —

DAVE. I warned you. Did I not say I'd kill you? *(Laura struggles and they move a semicircle. He pulls the belt tight with several jerks. Concentrating, his back to Ray. Ray reaches under the pillow, withdraws the hammer, walks over to Dave and hits him twice with the hammer. Dave instantly collapses and Laura struggles out from under.)*

LAURA. No! Christ no!

RAY. Evil fucker. You're *evil!* *(Ray hovers. Laura wrestles the hammer away.)*

LAURA. Ray!

RAY. Burn in hell. Yes, you. *Hell. (Pause. Ray looks at Laura then runs out. Laura stands there in shock.)*

LAURA. Oh, Jesus ... Jesus Mary and Joseph. *(She catches her breath then kneels down beside Dave, tries to turn him over but can't. Suddenly he stirs; she jumps to her feet.)* I'll ... call an ambulance.

(Dave struggles to get up, Laura picks up the hammer and fidgets with it watching Dave and dialing the telephone. He collapses again and tries to heave himself up. Laura drops the phone and watches Dave.) Stay where you are, Dave ... I'm warning you ...

Scene 7

Hospital. Laura and Pete sit on chairs in casualty. Pete smokes a cigarette.

PETE. I went in there. I went and saw this woman he's been seeing. Turns out he hasn't been seeing her-what am I talking about — I knew he hadn't been seeing her. They never even heard of him. I say, "How come you never heard of him?" They say, "Because he didn't fill out the form." "What are you talking about?" I say. "I filled out the form." "No, you filled out *your* form," they say. "He's supposed to fill out his form and take it to a different building." "I filled out the fucking form," I say. "I did everything to the letter." "No," they say, "you filled out the form to say he filled out his form. If he didn't fill out his form then it's null and void." *(Beat.)* Then they gave me more forms. Emergency forms or something. Review forms. They say it isn't too late for him to fill it in now, if he fills it in now and brings it back Monday they could help. If I can find him and be so good as to get a pen in his hand. What am I, a fucking magician? Where are these people who make the rules? Where are they hiding — can't they see what's happening? *(Beat.)* The man's lying in there with his brain stoved in. What are we gonna say? He ... beat himself to death? Just for the hell of it? He could've died ... We should tell somebody. Maybe we could explain.
LAURA. Explaining never got anyone anywhere. We'll explain he fell out of bed.
PETE. Laura —
LAURA. And down a flight of stairs. You'd be surprised what can

61

happen to a person falling out of bed.

PETE. He'll tell them!

LAURA. He's a fucking vegetable — how's he going to tell 'em?

PETE. If he comes round —

LAURA. He won't. *(Pause.)*

PETE. How do you know? He got a few whacks in the head a cracked skull they'll do this emergency operation and bob's your uncle.

LAURA. He got more than a few.

PETE. What d'you mean? *(Pause.)*

LAURA. He was trying to get up.

PETE. When?

LAURA. Later, later he tried to get up so I ... gave him a couple more is all. Just a tap. Here and there. *(Pause.)*

PETE. What are you telling me, Laura?

LAURA. I —

PETE. That between the two of you you just hammered this man half to death? That you and him just took it in turns ... hammering your boyfriend to ...

LAURA. He just tried to kill me. What's he gonna tell them?

PETE. I feel sick.

LAURA. Don't be such a baby.

PETE. No I do, I really ... I'm surrounded by maniacs. *(Long pause.)* I should go and ...

LAURA. Yes you go and ...

PETE. If I know Ray he's probably in the pub. What d'you think? That wouldn't surprise me.

LAURA. He won't be in the pub.

PETE. How do you know?

LAURA. Face it, Pete! *(Pause. Pete gets up.)*

PETE. Will you be all right ... I mean ... on your own? *(Pause.)*

LAURA. I want to be on my own. *(Pete exits. Lights down slowly on Laura.)*

Scene 8

Restaurant kitchen. Ray is wearing Pete's whites and chef's hat. He holds a rusty old petrol can and walks in a circle around the kitchen, carefully pouring. He finishes and sets the can down. Pats his pockets. Pete appears at the door silently, looking haggard and wearing Ray's old long coat. Ray doesn't notice him for a moment and Pete hasn't yet noticed the petrol.

RAY. You got a light?

PETE. What do you want a light for?

RAY. I got a few things here I want to set fire to.

PETE. What things?

RAY. Everything. *(Pete comes into the kitchen, sniffs with growing alarm, looks at Ray who produces a lighter and holds it up. Pete stops.)*

PETE. JESUS WHAT ARE YOU DOING?

RAY. This is where it all happens, isn't it, Pete?

PETE. This ... yes is where I work, Ray, you can't —

RAY. Yes and where Dad worked before you and I worked with him.

PETE. That's right, Ray —

RAY. In this kitchen here.

PETE. Yes.

RAY. Which is in this restaurant.

PETE. Yes, my restaurant! Everything/I own.

RAY. Which is in this family.

PETE. Yes, it's in the family!

RAY. I don't like families.

PETE. Well, they're all different/aren't they?

RAY. I wasn't good enough at doing the dishes so they sent me away.

PETE. No, Ray —

RAY. And I got sick because I wasn't strong enough.

PETE. You were sick because you were sick/there's no —

RAY. And then Dad killed Mum.

PETE. *(Beat.)* What?

RAY. It's true. He left her and then she died.

PETE. It was breast cancer.

RAY. She died because she wasn't strong enough.

PETE. She was very ill, sometimes that happens …

RAY. Dad wasn't strong enough either, was he?

PETE. *(Desperate.)* I don't know what you're talking about!

RAY. None of us was strong enough.

PETE. Ray, please!

RAY. None of us! This fuckin' family … it's cursed … marked!

PETE. Give me the lighter!

RAY. Damned. *(Ray catches his breath and hands Pete the lighter, as Pete takes it Ray whips another from his pocket and holds it up.)*

PETE. Jesus!

RAY. But you can cook, can't you, Pete?

PETE. Yes.

RAY. So let's cook! Uh? *(He upends the petrol can over his head, Pete covers his eyes in anguish.)*

PETE. NO!

RAY. Cook everything and make it worthwhile! Make it something that people want.

PETE. … You can't …

RAY. And need.

PETE. Please, I'm … begging you. *(Ray hands him the lighter quickly, Pete takes it and Ray withdraws another from his pocket.)*

RAY. You know what I think, Pete?

PETE. I have no idea.

RAY. I think I wasted my life. What are the chances of me getting a job in this gaff?

PETE. Well, Ray … this is a very small operation. I don't employ that many/people.

RAY. Yes but you could employ me! I'm your brother.

PETE. It doesn't work like that anymore. It wouldn't help. What would help is me running this place/successfully.

RAY. It would help me, you cunt!

PETE. I am helping you this is how I'm helping you! *(Ray tries to light*

the lighter. Pete makes a lunge at Ray and Ray dodges.) Christ, no, no!
RAY. I can't stand it, Pete! I just can't stand it anymore! *(Pete keeps his distance as Ray attempts to ignite the lighter, it won't light.)*
PETE. Leave it alone! *(He grabs hold of Ray. They wrestle over the lighter and Pete gets it.)* STOP!
RAY. I can't stop — get off of me! *(He breaks away, suddenly changing.)* What?! Shut up! Shut ... I'm, not listening. Jesus, no!
PETE. You ... you ... talk to me for fuck's sake. Tell me what it is. *(Ray has his hands clamped over his ears and is watching Pete. Silence. They catch their breath.)* It's the ... it's the voices, isn't it? *(Ray trembling, finally nods.)* They've come back. *(Ray nods.)* What are they saying?
RAY. They say ... all different things.
PETE. Like what? *(Pause.)* Come on, Ray, you can tell me. *(Pause. Ray produces another lighter from his pocket.)* Please ...
RAY. They say to me that I should ... go somewhere and ...
PETE. Go somewhere. Go where?
RAY. Go everywhere ...
PETE. Everywhere OK ...
RAY. And and find ... something although I don't know what it is.
PETE. Well, like what? *(Pause. Pete reaches out for the lighter slowly, Ray draws away slowly.)*
RAY. Find a way of stopping things happening.
PETE. What things?
RAY. Things like this obviously.
PETE. And?
RAY. Find a way of ... living with ... memory.
PETE. Memory yes ...
RAY. Cos that's what triggers it I'm sure. Or else ... signals from somewhere ... possibly the saucepans and the metal objects transmit signals but I can't be sure.
PETE. I doubt it.
RAY. Yes, but if we set fire to everything then if there were any transmitters they'd be ruined wouldn't they?
PETE. Let's just concentrate on the memories.
RAY. OK ...
PETE. What memories?
RAY. *(Beat.)* Like the time remember when we were kids ... when

65

things first started happening ... and Dad comes home and ... it's hot, a hot summer and we're walking down Fulham Palace Road on the big wide pavement and we're talking and I turn to look at him ... I just get a glimpse of him and ... I just notice how filthy he is and unshaven and how he stinks and he wears ... like an old blue safari suit ... and there are little specs of blood round the collar where he cuts himself shaving ... and his teeth, his eyes ... his eyes are brown, all of it brown even the white bits are brown. And I think ... I think ... I'll be like that one day. *(Pause. Dazed. Listening.)* They scare the shit out of me. They say very fucking weird things I can tell you. Things even too weird for you to figure out, Pete. I try to get real people to talk to me so I can compare the difference but it's not easy. *(Pause.)* What do they say to you?

PETE. I don't get them, Ray.

RAY. Oh. *(Silence.)*

PETE. But I know ... I know Dad had ... a bit of difficulty with things. He had a sort of ... faith ... in things which ruined him.

RAY. I don't have any faith, Pete. *(Beat.)* Some people just don't. *(Long pause. Pete takes the lighter from Ray gently.)* What's going to happen to me?

PETE. Nothing.

RAY. Nothing? Ever?

PETE. *(Gently.)* What do you want to happen?

RAY. I don't want the injections.

PETE. Nobody's giving you injections.

RAY. My four-weekly injections. They'll give me them after four weeks, they're like that. *(Pete puts an arm round Ray to comfort him.)*

PETE. Come on, it's OK.

RAY. I know it's OK but it doesn't seem OK and ... have you got a fag? *(Pete shakes his head.)* I just thought I'd ask but I understand if you don't. *(Pete pats him on the shoulder, drapes a couple of dish-cloths around him and carefully mops him dry as they speak.)* Because you don't smoke, do you, Pete?

PETE. Not normally no, no.

RAY. I got the lighters in King Street. I know that fellow who sells them, you know. I know that fellow. Six for a pound.

PETE. Bargain.

RAY. In Shepherd's Bush Market there's a fellow who sells real guns. Imagine that.

PETE. Real guns, really?

RAY. Yes for twelve pounds ninety-nine which is a bit steep.

PETE. For a real gun yes.

RAY. And monkeys. Real monkeys or at least very big bags of peanuts.

PETE. Well, that's wonderful.

RAY. Yes. Real monkeys. *(Pete takes his coat off and helps Ray into it.)*

Scene 9

A kitchen in a hostel. Ray and Pete are cooking on a portable hot plate. Pete chops and stirs, etc., while Ray looks on vaguely, sedated.

PETE. I got it in the market. It's quite neat. It's compact, see, and it doesn't use much power so if you — if you do accidentally set fire to anything you fling a blanket over it and the flames are contained. It's not much cop for fry-ups but if you want a plate of beans or a nice cup of warm milk to help you sleep it takes two minutes.

RAY. I thought gas was better.

PETE. It is better, but this is your own. Your own little cooker, you keep it in your room and you don't have to come out for anything.

RAY. They got gas here. I've seen it. Big, big hob.

PETE. Will they let you use it?

RAY. Dunno. *(He considers it and makes a face.)* You think of everything, Pete —

PETE. Yes I do.

RAY. You're a clever man.

PETE. You're a clever man too. *(He stirs a pan on the hot plate.)* Now. Onions.

RAY. Onions.

PETE. Always fry 'em in butter.

RAY. Yes.

PETE. Tastes better, gives it a better consistency. You come down and the pan's all dirty ('cos all this stuff's dirty) and you use margarine it'll go black and thin. Butter stays thick.

RAY. Got it.

PETE. Especially for soup.

RAY. Soup, right.

PETE. They get the tinned soups in here every week but if you wanna make your own or you wanna make a sauce, a nice pasta dish, you use butter or oil and the fats from the thing. From what you're cooking. Have a whiff. *(Ray sniffs at the pan.)*

RAY. Nice. What about eggs?

PETE. Fried eggs?

RAY. No, omelette.

PETE. In this instance yes we use butter.

RAY. Because it's better.

PETE. In this instance yes but just for an egg normally that can be expensive. *(Beat.)* Eggs aren't important. Eggs are eggs.

RAY. Everybody here likes fried eggs.

PETE. I don't often cook eggs. If I do, I don't fry 'em anyway. If I did, I wouldn't use butter. Just my preference.

RAY. 'Cos you're a businessman.

PETE. I'm a businessman, that's right. *(Pause.)*

RAY. Laura used to use butter.

PETE. Laura's not a businessman.

RAY. No and she's not a businesswoman either. She just used to cook sometimes.

PETE. That's different. If you cook for a friend then you go that extra mile. If you ever have any friends over to this place I'll bring you some butter.

RAY. Thank you.

PETE. My pleasure. *(He cooks.)* Now. Always put your onions in long before any garlic. Garlic burns too quick and you can fuck it up.

RAY. Onions beforehand.

PETE. That's right.

RAY. Long long before.

PETE. That's right.

RAY. How long before?

PETE. Till they go translucent.

RAY. It's ... an art, isn't it?

PETE. It's a very creative thing and it keeps your mind occupied. Feeding people is a serious business. Never use tinned tomatoes. Too watery and acidic. Use 'em fresh and always put 'em in last, very last so they don't disintegrate.

RAY. Disintegrate, yeh. *(Pause.)* Laura used to use tinned.

PETE. Well, it's not advisable.

RAY. It's cheaper. One time I saw them for twenty-three pee a tin. Tesco's.

PETE. Money isn't everything.

RAY. But twenty-three pee a tin, Pete ...

PETE. What d'you wanna put in now? *(Pause.)*

RAY. Did ... did you speak to her then?

PETE. Yes I did. What do you want — mushroom?

RAY. Eggs.

PETE. We're not ready for eggs yet. Eggs come last.

RAY. Mushroom then.

PETE. Mushroom. Now we are talking. *(Pete puts the mushrooms in.)*

RAY. What did she say? More mushrooms — what did she say?

PETE. *(Beat.)* Well ... it's not really very good news, Ray.

RAY. Mm-hm.

PETE. She's had a lot to cope with.

RAY. Mm-hm.

PETE. She says she wants to try and ... get herself together for a while. Get her life back together, for the kid maybe.

RAY. Can we put the eggs in now?

PETE. Not yet. *(Beat.)* She said she's actually quite happy on her own. She doesn't really want to ... threaten that. *(Ray nods. Pause.)* She ... she doesn't really want to see you again. For a while. *(Pause.)*

RAY. Not till she's feeling better.

PETE. No.

RAY. And ... and not till I'm feeling a bit better perhaps.

PETE. Not for a while.

RAY. Not for a long while no. How long?

PETE. She didn't say. I mean you can't really say, can you? *(Pause.)*

RAY. Roughly.

PETE. She said she didn't know.

69

RAY. What, she didn't have any idea at all?

PETE. I think maybe she might try and go home or something.

RAY. She won't go home.

PETE. She said maybe she might write to you ... in a few months.

RAY. How many months, six?

PETE. Six, maybe six, yes.

RAY. Six, OK. Six. *(Pause.)* Six months exactly or less?

PETE. It's just a guess, Ray. It could be less, could be a bit more ... When she's had the kid maybe.

RAY. Right. *(Pause.)*

PETE. I mean she's a nice girl Laura, but you ... you gotta remember she's got her own life to lead. And she did before you came on the scene and before the other guy and she'll do what she can to keep that life on track. It's the way people are.

RAY. Because ... we had a good time together. We understood each other.

PETE. I know but also you have your own life to lead too. You gotta think about yourself now. What you're gonna do with yourself.

RAY. I don't really want to think about that.

PETE. Well, it happens to the best of us. Sooner or later we're all on our own for a while. And then we're with someone again. And then we're alone again maybe. Swings and roundabouts. *(Pause.)*

RAY. She's very very beautiful, Pete. Did you notice that? I don't think I've ever met anybody as beautiful as that. I mean ... seriously, she's the type of girl you'd die for. People say they'd die for this person or for that person but I mean this time round I found out ... what they meant. She's the type you could hold in your arms and gaze at without even ... getting squeamish or anything. You could ... you could say you loved hear and have absolutely no regrets about it that's for sure. *(Beat.)* You'd love her all over, everything about her. Her face, her legs, her arms, her shoulders, her feet, her toes, breasts, hair, hands. *(Beat.)* Knees. Neck. Her laugh, she had a blindin' laugh, Pete, which was because of her eyes, she had very dark blue twinkling eyes. *(Beat.)* Her mouth. Her lips, lips like a duck's which — like this — which shows she's thoughtful, doesn't it, Pete?

PETE. Well ... I'm sure she's thinking about you, Ray. I'm sure you'll never stop thinking about each other.

RAY. No.

PETE. No. *(Long pause. Pete picks up a clump of basil and sniffs it, then hands it to Ray who also sniffs it.)* When you chop the basil, always use more than you think you'll need. It grows on trees so use it like it grows on trees. Be generous with it. *(Beat. Ray nods.)* You have a go. *(Ray takes the knife and chops the basil carefully. Pete watches as he sprinkles it into the pan. Lights down slowly. Blackout.)*

End of Play

PROPERTY LIST

Suitcase (RAY)
Piece of paper, pen (RAY, IVES)
Four-pack of beer (RAY)
Phial of pills (PETE)
Money (PETE, DAVE)
Brick (DAVE)
Sticking plaster, Band-aids (LAURA)
Plates of food (PETE)
Cigarette, drink (LAURA)
Drinks (RAY)
Bag of chips (LAURA)
Wrapper (RAY)
Cigarettes, lighter (RAY and LAURA, DAVE, PETE)
Shopping bags, beer can (IVES)
Blanket, picnic food, wine, four-pack of beer (RAY and LAURA)
Pillow (LAURA)
Hammer (LAURA, RAY)
Purse (LAURA)
Bottle in brown paper bag (DAVE)
Ring (DAVE)
Lunch, beer, wine (RAY and LAURA)
Blankets, papers (RAY)
Towel (DAVE)
Gas can (RAY)
Lighters (RAY)
Dishcloths (PETE)
Portable hot plate, pan, spoon, knife, food (PETE and RAY)
Mushrooms (PETE)
Basil (PETE)

SOUND EFFECTS

Spanish guitar music
Intercom
Bar music
Phone ringing